Less Like a Dove

Agi Mishol

Less Like a Dove

*translated
from Hebrew by
Joanna Chen*

Shearsman Books

First published in the United Kingdom in 2016 by
Shearsman Books
50 Westons Hill Drive
Emersons Green
BRISTOL
BS16 7DF

Shearsman Books Ltd Registered Office
30–31 St. James Place, Mangotsfield, Bristol BS16 9JB
(this address not for correspondence)

www.shearsman.com

ISBN 978-1-84861-476-5

Contents

Introduction

I first got to know Agi Mishol through a slender book of poems, *Wax Flowers*, in which Mishol explores her relationship with her dead parents. My mother was dying at the time, and I carried the book in my bag like an amulet. The immediacy and down-to-earth quality of Mishol's poetry spoke directly to me: the way she infuses her poems with both humour and jarring realism; the way her meditations overflow with the raw countryside around her.

Some months later, we met at her home in a village in central Israel. I left after several hours of warm conversation, my arms full of the many books Mishol has published both in Hebrew and other languages, my heart full of a desire to dig deeper into her words.

Although Mishol does not regard herself as a political poet, her poetry is infused with the politics of Israel and the dichotomies within it. "We're not sitting in the Himalayas meditating — we're sitting here in turmoil in this mad, aggressive country and the politics percolates, seeps into my poetry," Mishol said in one of our many discussions about the impossibility of protecting poetry from politics.

Well attuned to the complicated evolution of the Hebrew language, Mishol moves seamlessly from Biblical Hebrew to contemporary Hebrew slang, often in the same stanza. The historical, cultural and social connotations implicit in Mishol's words provide a challenge. The writer Cynthia Ozick suggests that "translation can serve as a lens into the underground life of another culture," and my wish while translating was to create this lens for readers of English.

The poetry of Mishol is evocative, accessible, grounded in the present yet steeped both in Mishol's personal past and in the public past of Israel. The lyricism of her poems nestles within a language that is colloquial and familiar. Despite the simple diction, the challenge for me was to translate the words without removing them from their larger cultural context and also to preserve the gentle lyrical quality that Mishol's poetry possesses in the original Hebrew. Most of all, to open her world to others.

JOANNA CHEN

The Sermon at Latrun

You piss on my love as if
it were a bonfire, extinguishing it
ember by ember with the arrogance
of the perfect crime, and afterwards
you cry at night in front of an empty robe,
a shirt on a barbed wire hanger –
What were you thinking?

So your carriages turned into pumpkins,
your horses to mice,
and rags began peeping through.
Both of you, covered in fig leaves,
biting into the apple of knowledge,
knowing how to enter and exit the norm –
Were you not afraid?
Did you never hear that God
has no God?

You will be wanderers in the cash flow
of life, dogs without collars.
You will never relax into form,
never again hear the heart go boom –

A pig's head resting on a tray,
a green apple stuffed in its mouth –
With this you remain –
So sayeth the Lord.

Betrayal

All the sorrel stalks I sucked on
revealed nothing.

Words piled up behind my back
until they turned into a green hill.
Phloem coursed through the trunks;
lupine seeds plotted blue in the dark soil.

Even if there is no singular form for grass
and only the plural makes it green,
I could not have known.

Birnam Wood began to move,
afterwards thought darkened
with everything that lay behind the trees.

Night Lamp

It takes time for the body
to grasp what the mind has decided
so the body strokes itself
with an outline of consolation:
here the shoulder, here
the face, here the inner thighs –

This is the bottomless sigh
devoid of a consonant
to lean against.

No Casualties Reported

No one counted him,
the little donkey
in the photograph
below the headlines.

A white donkey,
his life shackled to scrap iron
and watermelons,
who surely stood still
as they strapped the saddle
of dynamite to his body,
until they patted his behind
spurring him on with a *yallah itlah*
to the enemy lines –

Only then
mid-road
did he notice the pale grass
sprouting between the rocks
and he strayed
from the plot
in order to munch,
belonging only to himself
in the ticking silence.

It was not written who fired:
those who feared he would turn back
or those who refused the approaching gift

But when he rose to heaven
in a blaze
the donkey was promoted
to the rank of explosive messiah
and seventy-two tender virgin donkeys
licked his wounds.

Showing You

Undressing for you down to my handwriting
down to the gutturals
the hard phonetics
the vowels

until you see my O
my suffixes

the trees
pulped into
paper, flutes and a desk
with a chair that swivels
empty

when I come to you
so you will read my ink.

My Father Speaks Again

Let's see, you probably remember
how you followed my gurney
with a blue plastic cup containing my teeth,
my strength.

Your cries, searching for words,
collapsed into Hungarian stresses
and a doctor called Winker whistled to himself
a morning tune.

As he covered my body with a faded sheet
from Public Health I remembered
how you also got a glimpse when
you were three.

Your little eyes, with only cows
for comparison,
saw teats full of milk
dangling between my legs.

My Mother Adds

In my condition I can't remember
what I wanted to say to you
but I birthed you all
bones blood and milk.

And it hurts me to see you –
blue hair, golden eyes
still clambering out
of the abyss of my eyes
like a stubborn spider on webs of spittle
that you weave so well
with all the words you need
to invent for yourself
instead of me.

For Now

The days resemble one another.
The cat's sharp claws rest
deep within her paws.

In the yard the dogs
gnaw on a rabbit's skull.
My shadow extends, grows

long. At night the stars exit
their kennel. I listen to the barking
but have no answer.

Spring is putting on its makeup
under the soil.

Holocaust, Remembrance, Independence

How we flew –
Not from Gadera to Rehovot or up the Castel
en route to Jerusalem, like in those dreams, but
outside of the stratosphere: my father, myself
and that blurry one called Agnes,
who in nineteen fifty changed her name
to Agi, and since then this hollow girl has tailed
my father, who was her father as well.

We flew –
Not like *Haaretz* newspapers that land every morning,
spreading their flimsy wings on the table,
but forking with swimming motions beyond the stratosphere
until we suddenly dove, wings compressed,
into an air pocket, Europe revealed to us
and afterwards, deserts and seas.

Had I not flown I would have put off my shoes
in the name of my skilled body, remembering its movements
still in chaos after climbing, ascending like a lizard
from the waters while still a bird,
taking off through clouds to slash across an entire continent.
Now I have touched I can never forget,
and even if from afar we look like swallows
copulating as we glide,
we are just a father and daughter.

He pushes me on with his dolphin snout,
covers me with a clown's costume

so no one will peek at
the mother in me.

And I, Agi Mishol, second generation,
light these flames of words
that are not weapons and do not deter.

Geese

Epstein, my math teacher,
liked to call me to the blackboard,
said my head was more suited to hats,
and that a bird with brains like mine
would fly backwards.
He sent me to tend geese.

Now, years away from that verdict,
I sit under the palm tree
with my three beautiful geese,
thinking he was farsighted,
that teacher of mine.
He was right,

because nothing makes me happier
than to watch them now,
falling upon bread crumbs,
wagging their tails joyfully,
or freezing for a moment
under beads of water
when I spray them
with a hose,
holding their heads high,
bodies stretched back
as if remembering faraway lakes.

My math teacher is long gone,
together with the problems
I never solved.

I like hats
and in the evening,
when the birds return to the trees,
I look for the one flying backwards.

GPS Directions to My House

Exit the highway and continue straight until the circle
of three olive trees. You are looking for Kfar Mordechai,
although you have no idea who Mordechai is and why a village
would be named after him. In another hundred metres, turn left.
Turn left.

To your right, bundles of hay on their way to bread.
Open the window, smell the damp of stubble.
An optimist with earphones jogs by the side of the road.
Overtake him, elbow hanging out the car window,
until the T-junction where peacocks stroll.
Turn right.

Now the sun is behind you although better to see it
filling the wing mirror with orange. As you cross
the Sorek river at the magical hour of photography,
of feather clouds and scented creepers, your mood
changes; the sight of red roofs covering the houses
arouses an orphan's yearning within you.

It is easy to get to me from here, even in neutral,
freewheeling towards the sign "Mishol", where
dogs greet you, barking, but also wagging their tails,
and before you get out of the car you must decide
which end to believe.

Mother Tongue

The neighbour who pulled me out,
who cut me away from you,
likely said: *It's a girl!*
I gulped you down
right away, searching
for myself
on the snowy screen
of your eyes. My father
meanwhile accompanied
a silent movie on an old piano
in a cinema.
An autumn sun was shining
in Szilagycseh.
In exchange for a goose,
a gypsy revealed I would see far
but no one understood
the prophetic *ahh*,
the lingering aleph I screamed into the room.
Later you shrivelled into a thumb
that became an eraser
atop a pencil
that I sucked on until I turned it
around and began to write
poetry
that returned to me
as mother.

Grain of Wheat

There is nothing more whole than a broken heart
Rabbi Menachem Mendel of Kotsk

I'm not used to sleeping with others
because my soul shifts position
and come morning I need to be left
alone. Perhaps the heart is broken
but do not jump to conclusions.
With all respect to the Rabbi
of Kotsk, there is something
more whole than a broken heart
and like an ant I know how to descend hell
with a measuring tape made of straw,
and come back with a grain of wheat.

Love Reports for Reserve Duty

With full military armour
and secret password
love issues herself a call-up
into a midnight dream,
spraying the room with
the semen-scent of carob blossom.

Go, I tell her.
The wars are over.
And before you get the hell out,
write me one hundred times:
Forgive me for revealing myself
to you in the body of a deserter.

Post-Coital Blues

Post coitum omne animal triste est
            Galen, 2nd Century Greek physician

Not merely sad.
Some keep sobbing
without understanding why,
emitting unexpected cries
like lamented gurgles
or wails
after the two-backed beast
has split asunder, and out of nowhere
a wall appears between them, even a transparent one,
and a sudden fall back onto the sheets
from the heights of lost consciousness
hurls them back into themselves like
the end of a movie when
the lights go up –

*

Let us not forget
that most of them were sad
to begin with, before this grace of forgetfulness
from which no one knows where
to turn –

*

But not all of them.
Some just lie back and rise up
harmoniously
listening to the body cells vibrating,
no hidden seams or folds,
no wish to move to never-land.

*

Not all of them are sad.
Some of them lie
in the soft grass,
staring at the sky through the
pine cones until a playful wind
fluffs up their feathers,
moving the green and
reminding them that even when the
heart suddenly empties out –
the world is always full.

Rings

The first was the most determined –
simple silver,
three violet stones,
direct hit to the finger.

The second was of gold,
slender as a hint,
four drops of pigeon blood
dripped across it.

The third, of sapphire, opened
its Cyclops eye;
six amethyst leaves turned it
into a bouquet of a single flower.

And there was a fourth.

From rope.

Between the Trees and the Non-Trees

I go nowhere,
too decrepit to be uprooted
or taken out of context.
My laziness stays put,
settling down in familiar space
as evening falls
on the steps,
imagination sated,
my hunters' eyes already
resting in the sockets of my brain.

Why get up, why come
and go, why stir things up
for a perfumed orchard
whose breath I breathe –

Palm fronds wipe clean
the sky's windscreen
of words that cling when love has gone.
One by one ravens merge into
cypress trees like blood
into silence.

Thought does not covet
its contents.
I am simply here
between the trees and the non-trees
my door open wide,
the soft night invited home.

from Wax Flowers

1.
I do not know you
to tell the truth
you do not know me either.

I see the rusting wire in your eyes
and your ailing soul in the evening
with a small tuna salad in your lap
together with toast
in front of the TV.

But your mother tongue is not mine,
so we prefer to stroll:
walking is better than sitting,
sitting better than lying down,
lying down better than sleeping.

And we stroll,
your arm strung through mine,
and we play once upon a time I
was your mother,
and now you are mine.

2.
I didn't have to snitch to 999
I could have smuggled you
off to my veterinarian
could have put you to sleep
away from here

Could have cradled
your head and whispered good girl good girl
until the contractions of death ended
as long as it took
for you to birth yourself
through to the other side.

3.
Each morning I bring you
pretty little homemade sandwiches
so you'll have
beautiful words of bread
to pacify Mr. Death:
oatmeal,
sprouts,
I bring you
pumpernickel, seven-grain bread
if only you'd eat,

eat fresh bread against death
whole wheat against emptiness.

4.
Through the door frame
she too is trapped in neon time –
an old lady with no panties
talking to God.

Actually she's addressing a dove
squashed in the concrete crevice
of a hospital window.

White dove.
Perhaps take pity on your neighbour
exhausted
fluttering now
beyond the curtain
between the cymbals of electricity
conducted by a doctor on duty.

5.
At night in my bed
I fulfil your wish
to lie on your side with bent knees.
Afterwards in a dream I sink into
your brown angora sweater
soft as love
simple as a peanut.

6.
In the death announcements
they stuck you near a doctor.
Even now, after leaving
this world,
he still carries his ghostly title
and you, finally,
get to lie next to a doctor.

7.
It was a modest ceremony:
The Interior Ministry clerk handed me
your graduation certificate. You
who never had any certificate,
never won anything,
suddenly won a beautiful certificate of
death with a state emblem.
As if you had excelled at something
and passed all the tests.

She asked if I want to update
(so she said) my father's death certificate.
Afterwards she laid them side by side
like matching gravestones
and pressed an electric buzzer.

I went down the street and kept walking
like a child,
a small one
holding hands with paper parents
who rustle in the wind.

Back Then

When we loved without margins and God
came to take his due, we threw him a faint smile, thinking he
deserved
no more.

Long distance gazers, we put our trust in cakes of love
little fried crêpes
of lust
for the seven
good years

forfeiting wings that
grow
only to those who first jump
into the abyss
without them.

This Is What We Do

We live in a hermetic present
on a hen's forked legs

and the road not taken
lives on inside us

without us ever knowing
where it ends.

The damp stain on the sheet
is the repeated death

of our children
and before sleep

we have only one sheep
to count.

We each wake up
in our own bodies

so sensitive to the shape of the air
between objects

and the x-rays of sunlight
between the poplar leaves.

We drink love
like camels.

We do our best
to happen

before the end casts
its icy die

into the heart.
This is what we do.

Ostrich (The Poet Leafs Through Drafts)

He created the ostrich out of leftovers and whatever he could
not
say was good.

He created it at the end of a particularly
difficult day, exhausted and
distracted.

It was dark, the creatures rushed around
and he had no energy to start anything new.

He attached goat legs to chicken toes
that were a bit too big
and on blushing thighs assembled a bird's torso
in a black feathered skirt.

He admits:
the proportions recalled a draft
of something he didn't have the power to bring
to completion:

The wings for example can't bear the body's weight
(how focused he was when creating the pomegranate)
and the head, if you can so call a beak and pair of eyes,
is simply a place where the neck
that is too long (what the heck)
loses its name.

Maybe because of this he felt the need
to compensate it with some world records:

Aside from the fact it's the largest bird
on planet earth and the swiftest
of all creatures on two legs
and its feathers adorn hats and boas
and its eggs are used as bowls
that can also be fashioned into lampshades –

He awarded it
(totally defying protocol)
the metaphor of the head stuck in the sand.

Working Order

You were right, some were exiled
from their homelands by the god
of notebooks to write his biography.
Most of us are assigned some small turf,
multiplying his eyes, while others digress.

He placed Mary Oliver by a black pond
to cultivate and keep it.
He embedded Tranströmer in the northern snows
and Sirkka Turkka with her dogs
deep in the forest right under the smoke.

At times he conceded, allowing Pessoa
to wander from persona to persona
inside himself.

Some he fuelled in saloons,
bestowing upon Po or Cavafy
a trampoline of gutters.

Others he diluted in metropolitans,
reserving them tables in cafes
because only there could
his solitude touch theirs.

He gave comfort to the Irish
with beautiful potatoes
laid by the ground in their honour.

Me, he dropped (held in the hands
of parents from an inferno)
into a shaded persimmon grove
under the migration track of birds.
Ravens see me exiting
and entering the house,
caw-cawing.

The Short Story Competition

The brain announces a short story competition.
It changes from day to day, depending on the threshold
of pain, but the opening line is always the same:
There is no way back to what we were.

The stories are similar,
many written at night to the sounds
of jackals and owls,
considering the fate of love
that plummets to below zero
and becomes a mirror image of itself.

Some highlight turning points
with a thick marker; in others
they are engulfed by the regular continuum
of a stream of consciousness.
Instead of writing,
some circle the lack with blue chalk
like a corpse removed from a crime scene.

The cunning ones try to prove
that you can bathe twice in the same river.
Wise guys steer the plot
to alternative places,
while others try squeezing
under the locked door
through a thin ribbon of light.

There are no judges
and no winners.

The painful place continues
to shatter against cliffs of common sense
in a furious torrent of manes and cockscombs,
continuously deleting the final paragraphs
like a wicked editor,
leaving a shore as smooth
as a page.

May Song

Chickens come.
I throw stale bread
and watch them peck.
The cat comes too,
sits and purrs.
This is a simple song –

The Pisardi plum I planted years ago
blossoms for the first time.
Butterflies fly around it
in pairs.
The dog comes too,
watching me with eyes like hearts.
I wish I was as worthy
as she thinks me to be.

A single red poppy
fires up the green.
How long will it take
for you to evaporate
from within me?

Parting from the dead is easier.

Writing

Writing is the tangled path
to love.

To live for it
is to rise and fall from the D Minor scale
of childhood
seams exposed
microphone aimed at the temples,

To hover over words
until they become a door
and then to burst through it
like fractals of broccoli,

To adjust the eyes
from 2 to 3D
until the letters scatter
bowing to each other
with the meekness of time
into the face of eternity.

To live for it
is to drop out of the sky
with the blazing trail
of a wish that belongs
to no one.

Lament

Woe to the man
who shot another
and killed himself.

Woe to gaping jelly eyes
of a fish sealed
in cling wrap, trembling
like the surface of the water.

Woe to the man
who wobbles on one leg by
an etching of a ship
like a sick heron,
in a house that has become
a mausoleum.

Woe to the woman
with the raven tattooed
on her heart
who now covers her head
until it turns into a room made of pashmina
and places a finger to her lips as if
it were the hole of the high C
on a flute.

Memo (1)

You do not have to pull out weeds
just because they are not flowers.
And before you pick up a stone
remember it is also a roof.

It is sad to see you crawling along
with a trail of yearning spittle,
writing these poems
as the sun sets, forgetting
that only nature is entitled
to kitsch like this.

Advice

Take a breath and pull away:
to the moon,
to Mars,
to the galaxies,
the milky halo of dark matter.

Once there, make your way back slowly:
Cassiopeia,
the tail of the Little Bear
oceans, continents,

the Earth,
spread with a layer of mankind,
buzzing with electricity.

Then, on a wooden chair
in your room,
repeat to yourself:
my words were taken out of context.
I was misquoted.

Fly on a Wall

A fly on a wall sees a woman
whose fingers look to her like
chicken legs. She is sleeping,

her dead panties chucked on a chair.
A passing cat sniffs and continues
its journey.

Whoever marked her with a ring no longer worries
about the path
of her flight.

In the Name of the Mother

I see you again tonight
fighting sleep with pillows and down comforters
a book slammed shut next to the bed.
You long ago stopped feeling
the pea under the mattress.

Your bad spirit has devoured you,
your fingertips are bitten,
the edges of your mouth turned down
as if you had eaten something sour.

You did not interpret the look in my eyes,
maybe because I have faded, my son,
hanging in a frame by your bed
for so long.

A woman is not a plank
you can cling to
with all your might
in order not to drown.

A body is not flesh
you can pitch a stake in,
erect a tent over,
or swallow at night
to dull the pain.

A woman is not a feather
in a tail spread out

for an imaginary audience
just to impress
yourself.

Even she cannot
remove the hands of the clock
from time, my son.

In fact, I liked the one
who dovetailed so well with your soul.
I never thought you deserved anything more
than love.

Green Things

They sit each side of a poem
as it were a crystal ball.

They ignite electricity between words and see
in the second stanza a praying mantis
wondering if it's worth giving up its head
for a quick screw.

The green, glistening pea
of Gmail
signifies they're both available

and never forget there's also an apple in the worm
because idioms always reinforce the opposite.

To: cherubatthegate@gmail.com

Quit with the sword for a minute,
put the blaze down,
fold the wings,
don't be such a seraph.

Here, I'm in.
I'm out.
Big deal.

Sent from my iPhone

Memo (2)

When you prayed, you talked
without stopping.
Now it's your turn to listen:
Nothing will be deciphered
through this threadbare cloth of words,
these domino letters collapsing backwards.
You should know already there are
no straight lines in nature, particularly
on the horizon where earth meets sky –
all hills and protrusions. These
rules govern you, too. Remember,
before you get sucked up
into the poem,
that spring begins in yellow,
when two-winged sprouts
lift up the earth's crust
with a strength reserved only
for the gentle.

Synchronicity

A person bangs his head against a wall
as cobwebs loosen around
a dead spider.

A person lies
in the hollow of a carton
with all the other eggs
improving relations with his
internal organs
and there are runners running in the body
that one day will turn around to kill him
and they are rushing nowhere
like hamsters on a treadmill
in the gym and
they say to the air: I'm on my mobile.

But there is also a she who anoints her body
and dedicates it to love
and a he whose soul bursts out towards her
less like a dove
more like a flower.
So here's to the salamanders
to the rays of light groping in the dark
and to all the erect double headstones.

Meeting

You look a bit like your dog who from one end
barks at me and from the other – wags its tail
and I don't know which to believe:
your smiling mouth or sad eyes,
the girl's demeanour peeking out of that face of yours
or voice of yolk that has dropped to bass clef.

How we envied ourselves back then;
all our affairs hid the emptiness perfectly,

threads from our own lifeline stretched out
to the sixth dimension where all possibilities exist,
and come morning there isn't always someone
to tell the dream to.

Husbands turn into relatives and the dead
live within us in so many forms.

Although we are not the screenplay of our lives
even acting is sometimes
beyond our power.

The closest thing we have to a mother
is a comforter to which we return
every evening like big fetuses,
dependent on their own body heat,

and even if the only umbilical cord is the wire
of the telephone, how good it is to talk,

how good it is that the blessed mind of morning
still grows out of the page.

Visiting Naomi

Von Weisel Convalescent Home, Gadera

1.
Here you are.
They put you out
in the garden
in a wheelchair.

You with the legs that buckle
still tangoing with your heart.

They put you in the sun
by a lizard
in a straight line
with the others
but without the firing squad.

2.
You want me to cover your face
because the eyelids are too scanty
because a hundred white eggshells
are marching together towards you
barefoot without shoes
because the sly dead are uncomfortable in their graves
and from time to time one appears in the image of another
relying on the fact you won't notice the difference now
when all your wakefulness is rapid eye movement.

3.
You drink coffee
to mark time:

Up to here;
from here.

4.
All the books
all the wisdom crowded on the shelves
all the philosophers, the poets –
lie silently one with the other
separated by cardboard dividers
under sheets of dust
in your house, your empty house.

5.
Surrounding you – wrapped in a bird
life leaps from branch to branch

Couples hatch out of beds
and drink Mighty Leaf tea.

People make time in their schedules
nodding vigorously

And you –
nothing
you want the nothing
towards which you are led
by a blind guide dog.

Reincarnation

It is hard for you to believe in reincarnation
but you are willing to try,
considering the alternative.
If only someone would explain to you
where the soul resides – in a city, a village
or a mere encampment,
and how much one can count on a soul
whose entire existence is based on rumour.

I read to you from *The Tibetan Book of the Dead*
on the journey of the soul to city, village or
that same encampment,
how it rises out of the body like a dove.

Tibetans make you laugh
but no matter.

What interests you is the precise moment when it all ends,
how from one moment to the next
blood and heart freeze inside the body
yet everything continues as if nothing has changed.

My dear, you are touching ninety
and know how to separate death
from fear of death.
When you snooze in your armchair
a breeze ruffles the pages of your book
and moves on.

You, too, can still watch a bird,
forget you are you,
become its flight.

Even the hard-wooded fist
of pine cone I saw outside
relaxed in the end, releasing kernels
to earth.

Silence

I am the silence of the room.
The thinner I am
the thicker the noise in your heads.

I breathe life in the words
that come.

I am the gaping hole
covered with a word.

You cannot escape me,
I am the quiet in the unquiet
of your bodies.

I lie in wait for you
after the cracking of knuckles,
the giggling and chuckling,
the wriggling in your seat.

I am what you bite
from the tips of your fingernails.
In me you meet
the ceiling,
the walls,
strange shapes that appear
out of floor tiles.

I am the attentiveness found all over,
rising out of you now.

Immobility

A male tortoise who rapped
on the back of a female
dropped
in the middle of pleasuring
and lies now
on his back
his four legs running
in the air.

He's a goner
until someone
absolves him.

Rabbit

Small rabbit
trapped in the glare
dazzled by the beam –

For you I will switch off the headlights
and drive in darkness.

Offering

It was only the tail
a long, dead tail
that the cat left on the mat
at the entrance.

Now she basks in the sun
licking her paw,
passing it across
her face,
very proud of the offering
laid at my door.

I pick up the tail
that will never move again
wrap it in paper
and thank her very much.

I enter the house
so as not to offend
and bury it, slowly,
in the trash.

The Candy Stand

Last night Mr. Grandy's candy stand
appeared in my dream.

Cups glowed like planets
around fountains of soda (red and green).
The pink fragrance struck at my heart,
returning me to childhood.

Banana-fish candy lay in rows
covered with forever-powdered sugar;
licorice fish (I could never decide
whether I liked them or not)
slowly blackened next to them.
Most of all, my tongue desired
the heads of the red sugar roosters
at the edge of rustling cellophane.

Mr Grandy, Lord of all
these treasures:
for years your traffic light candy
tempted me layer after layer
down to the core
and here I am,
standing on tiptoe, coins in hand,
reaching out to the candy.

Lord of cats' tongues,
you ask me what I want.

If only you knew how far away
my life would take me from the
magic candy counter
and how your question
entangled my soul.

She-Dog

1.
When she sees me in the morning
coming out of the house towards the fields
she leaps around me leaving
on the path
one long, precise sentence
on happiness.

2.
Proud of her name
she charges into the crows
just to prove she's guarding
the yard.

3.
She returns with a chicken in her mouth.
It must have escaped the neighbour's coop.
She won't eat it, but neither will she let it go,
just stands there steaming with the bird between her teeth
and a shy wag of her tail –
half she-dog, half she-wolf
lost on the border.

4.
She has no money
no clothes
and doesn't hold a grudge.

When she's hungry – she eats.
When she's thirsty - she drinks.
When she's tired she stretches out,
falls asleep under a bush.

5.
Always by my side
she goes where I want to
before I even get up.

Asana

All in all
it's about
liking or not liking,
and when mosquito thoughts
pierce sucking straws into flesh
return
to breathing –
the transparent elevator
that drops
within you
from floor
to floor.

Wrap one hand around a pen and the other on the key
to the heart
until you are a silver spoon –
a bowl
for soup

until you open your home to the night
like a blind person
who has no need
to turn on the light.

Courvoisier

Maybe because of the cognac she rips
the hair from his lower belly
with her toes

suddenly awakening the monkey in them, clinging to branches
so as not to fall into the gaping mouth of the lion
below.

A Kind of Wake-Up

Last night I snored as if drowning
no strength to grab
from inside myself
the thing
that rose up and sank
like an elevator growling
in the dark.
The cats sat
and listened.
One of them
put an end to it and
licked my armpit
with prickly tongue.

Something

Something
a certain sound
someone from the clouds who sings
I'm singing in the rain or
Arminda Canteros
playing tango on an old piano
from a disc
reminded me
that it was me
me that I forgot
the one under the crows
beside the yellow rose.

Back Home

Blessed is the light in the window,
Blessed is the generous tongue of the dog
and its tail of pure happiness.
Blessed are you, the match,
enabling a fire the length of a toothpick.
Blessed is the notebook I lean over,
naked.
Blessed are the holes around which no bagel twists,
blessed is the bed with its comforting burrow,
blessed is Simone Weil
and all who at this moment purify
the dead.

My Dog Libby

The old dog has forgotten who she is.
Can't hear, can't see, only her nose
quivers at the tail of a scent.

She stands in the middle of nowhere
like a stone, a tree,
a fence – can't hear, can't see,
her legs already buckling but
forgetting to sit.

"Circling," said the vet –
revolving aimlessly
demented like humans,
he explains.

The switch of her life is under my finger
but I can't be sure whether it is she who suffers
or I.

So I just stroke her head
and go visit
the woman whose life switch is under the finger
of someone else.

Translation

The siren caught us
with open dictionaries,
searching for the name of
a flower in English,
the Wandering Jew.

We did not know what to do:
run to the shelter or keep
translating. We laughed
and panicked in the same
language.

for Joanna Chen

Sing in Me, Muse (One Prayer and Two Answers)

PRAYER

Come see how beautifully
I've aligned myself for you,
standing with the cypresses,
wearing socks of lime wash.

The windows and the doors
are open wide,
eliminating the border between
field and house. Come,

the dust here does not change its name
to dirt,
no broom rises up
to the cobwebs.

From your safe place
you see a glimmer of white
moving through mallow leaves,
then you see the whole heron. Come,

I wait for you like a white-aproned
lapwing on toothpick legs
facing the sun,
praying for something –

ANSWER I

It's like this:
You sit on your cushion

eyes closed, opening
the lotus of your crown like a
funnel towards the light –
Double life, what were you thinking?
You with the pink uvula –

snap dragon mouth opening at my touch,
roaring like a fish,
what anaesthetized you like that?

Can't you hear the premature phrases
calling for intensive care from the pages?

When a word is held out
and you wear it on your chest,
orchestrated by your pulse,
does it not move you?

My sad field reporter,
my visual nerve,
no one drops out of the sky here.

Your own body that walks
through orchards of burning bushes
will rise up tomorrow to kill you.
So rise up and glide,
you, sleeping at the screen.

ANSWER 2

One more thing:
You lean into the soul
like men lean into car engines,
chewing on pencil stumps,
transporting commas from place to place
on days of grey matter.

You rummage through peanuts
and cheap TV shows again,
falling into bed with a Cadbury bar,
covering yourself with words that jar.

Uncurl yourself
from your hole.
This is a spot test
for May vipers
with triangular heads
and forked tongues,
loaded with ink,
about to inject the page.

Farm

There will be no peacocks strutting around
my yard. It was enough this morning
when I raised my ruddy face,
too ruddy for my taste,
from the sink to the bathroom mirror,
saw my honey-blond hair,
my sweet angelic curls.
God, how sugary I have become.
So no peacocks.

I'll get myself a pig
so I can say brand new sentences like
Go check on the pig or
The price of pigs
has gone up.
But no peacocks.

Now I'm the pig from the previous stanza,
lying on its back in a puddle of insult.
You can shove
You're my sunshine, my cream bun,
my cheese on toast
because words are one thing
and you are another.

I am the nice hedgehog
puffed up into a porcupine,
a menacing one that purples
and doubles itself

in the pupils of our eyes.
I am the metallic green fly
rubbing its legs in your face,
plotting against you,
even if the sorrel begins to babble
Spring behind my back,
gossiping about my impressionistic life
and the clean pink I open to the world
when I yawn.

Epilogue

It was a perfect murder
this side of the butterfly effect,
the bejewelled words
emptied of their flame.

Monsters of the imagination
no longer vex me with their boo-hoo.
It's just me and my laptop:

I hit *delete forever.*

Are you sure?

I hit *Yes.*

I am sure.

Snapshot

This backside revealed suddenly
in a mirror facing
a mirror
in the bathroom of a hotel
in a foreign city –
no one here
but me –
it must be mine:

pale moonscape
with furrowed craters
and hills of cellulite
that I land on
for the first time and plant
a flag.

Acknowledgements

Grateful acknowledgments to the editors of the publications where the following poems first appear, at times in earlier forms:

Asymptote: 'The Sermon at Latrun', 'Night Lamp' and 'Betrayal'.

The Bakery: 'My Father Speaks Again', 'My Mother Adds', 'Something' and 'My Dog Libby'.

The Blue Lyra Review: 'She-Dog'

The Ilanot Review: 'Wax Flowers' (1,4 and 7).

Liberation: New Works on Freedom from Internationally Renowned Poets: 'No Casualties Reported' and 'Mother Tongue'.

The Los Angeles Review of Books: 'Poets', 'Snapshot', 'Back Then', 'Showing You', and 'Synchronicity' excerpted in 'Figs and Facebook: The Poetry of Agi Mishol'.

Mantis: 'Ostrich (The Poet Leafs Through Drafts)' and 'Memo (2)'.

Poetry International: 'Snapshot', 'Advice', 'Betrayal'.